I'll Think of You

I'll Think of You

Reflections of Love
by Naomi Sheldon
Photographs by
Un Studio, Unltd.

♛ Hallmark Editions

I'll Think of You

Mary,

If I'm ever wondering what is love,
I'll think of how much I think of you.

And if I'm ever afraid
that I love too much, too soon,
I'll think of you then, too,
though I don't think it could
happen quite like that again.

I'll remember the night
I first saw you when you
had to leave with the girl
but came back to say,
How can I reach you?

I'll think of you on long
airplane trips to sad places,
and to happy places —
and when I see mountains, and
when the air smells of spruce.

*If anyone ever brings me
a book of poetry, I'll think
of you because you did.*

And if I ever ride a bike on a
dirt road, up and down hills
in the rain, I'll think of you —
riding with one hand,
a bottle of wine in the other.

When I'm aching from the
inability to communicate,
I'll think of you and how much
we cared and how deeply we felt
all those times when we
seemed to be strangers.

If I send or receive a telegram,
I'll think of you because
when I tapped a message
on your knee, though neither
of us knew the code, you
knew it said I Love You.

And when it's late and I'm alone
and about to get some fruit or tea,
I'll think of the night I was hungry
and went for some berries and
the phone rang before I could
wash them. It was you, and after
we hung up, I put the berries back
and went to sleep, warm and full.

*I'll remember your saying that
you wanted to love and be loved
but that you were afraid.
Your voice was lower and more
tired than usual.
I don't think I said a word.*

If ever I'm frustrated by bickering,
I'll think of when I trembled for us
after our first argument
and you said it was all right,
that we had to experience it
in order to get out of it.
And we promised to talk if it
happened again, if we were sad
or afraid. To talk and feel
instead of trying to hide from it
and ending up fighting—longing
for love, for understanding,
and fearing the longing.

And if I ever feel bad about talking too much, I'll remember that you don't mind, that you understand. When I need to talk, you talk as much as I by listening.

When I walk up long narrow
stairways, I'll think of you
walking ahead of me with your
arm behind your back,
your hand holding mine,
leading me to your home.

When I'm warm,
I'll think of you.

And when it's cold, I'll think of you.

When I'm feeling frightened,
I'll remember your saying Me Too.

And if I ever feel that bodies
are awkward and distant, I'll
remember how ours aren't.
How with us, touching is
no different from smiling.

When I hear the word Baby, sometimes so misused, I'll remember how you brought me to your chest, your arms around me, your hand on my head, and you called me Baby. It was the warmest thing I had ever heard.

Now when I play my guitar in the morning, I'll think of you asleep and smiling.

I'll remember that you kissed me goodnight on my lips gently as falling asleep. I had wondered if you liked me, and found out that you loved me.

Whenever I feel alone and scared, I'll remember how you in your sleep once sensed my fear, my inanimate trembling and sorrow, and you reached for me and held me, still asleep.

When I drink orange juice I'll think of you, toasting To Us at breakfast, our arms entwined.

When I drink Sangria,
I'll think of you.

If I'm ever sad because I'm
not loved, I'll think of you that
night at the concert saying
you were afraid to love me
because it would be so much.

And when I think of how
huge the world is,
I'll think of you and know that I exist.

*I'll think of you when I'm leaving
and have to think of what to say,
if something must be said,
so as not to say Goodbye.*

When I have a birthday,
I'll think of you.
And when I'm on a picnic.

And when I'm wondering if I'm
really alone, I'll remember
that finally I can be with you
and not have to touch you
to know you are there.

When I'm wondering what I am,
I'll remember the night, lying
beside you, I asked you if you
thought I was strange, and
you said no, I wasn't, that I
wasn't at all, and if you touched
me then, it was gentle,
and I believed you.

When I wake up in the morning
and don't remember the night
or my dreams, but just feel
warm and peaceful and deep,·
I'll think of you.

And if I ever think love is futile,
I'll think of you and know
that love is all that matters.
Futility is only a guess, a despair,
but love is everything
and worth all the risks.

I Love You!
Jim

Set in Jeannette, a light informal script
designed exclusively for Hallmark by Hermann Zapf.
Typography by Hallmark Photo Composition.
Printed on Hallmark Buff Vellux Paper.
Book design by Marjorie Merena.